JOB HUNTING THAT WORKS!

(FIND YOUR NEXT JOB IN A MONTH)

BY ANNA BOOTHE

This book is dedicated

With confidence

To my readers

Who are on their way

To new and rewarding jobs.

TABLE OF CONTENTS

INTRODUCTION

Unemployment, predicted to pass 10% nationwide and rising, is the number one problem in our current financial crisis. This is only those currently filing for unemployment claims and with the many who are no longer eligible or have given up, the number is probably twice that. And, even with the many thousands of jobs being made available by our national government, there is still no practical, no nonsense guide for the many, many workers who have been laid off through no fault of their own and who must find a job *NOW*, before next month's rent or mortgage is due to keep from becoming homeless as well as unemployed.

This is that guide, revised from a book by the same name that I published during the last recession which helped many find work, yes, in a month. I am an M. A. job counselor with experience with agencies including the Salvation Army, private employment agencies and finding jobs myself, always within a month. I have revised and updated this book for you, reflecting the massive layoffs we are experiencing, the many other problems we have including the mortgage crisis, the cuts in social services, bank and retirement fund failures and what seems to be a growing gloomy outlook for job hunters who may not have had to look for a job in years and suddenly are facing unemployment.

This book is for YOU—blue collar, white collar and professional—as the techniques are the same and time is of the essence for all since all are facing the same financial challenges and as applicants, we are all really in the same boat. Job cuts are occurring across the board in all sectors of our economy, with little or no notice and no time to waste.

This is a simple, straight forward guide that you can read the night before you start your job search and which will help you find a job in a month if you accept a few basic principles—you will accept any job that will meet your financial needs to survive (you may not be able to match the salary or benefits of the "career" you have had for years), you are willing to work full time every day to find your job and you are willing to use all the resources at your disposal, including you state employment office (necessary for unemployment benefits) and this book. And don't forget everything once you have a job but keep a low profile and really work at keeping it so you don't have to repeat this process again.

So if you just lost a job or think you are losing one, or want to make a change with the security you can get a job when you need it, this book is for you. Read carefully and give it your best effort. Then it will really be *Job Hunting That Works* for you!

Anna Boothe

SO YOU LOST YOUR JOB

Get over it!

This is not meant to be a harsh or unsympathetic remark but acknowledgment of reality and the first thing you must do if you are to find another job. I know this because I have lost many jobs and I can tell you first hand the first five are the hardest. Figures tell us that the average person changes jobs a dozen times in his forty plus years of employment so you have lots of company. I was in a field that offers many possible job titles and in which companies lay off people with no more concern than they change office equipment—in fact I often felt like a piece of office equipment in my jobs as a Gal Friday/clerk-typist/secretary/receptionist/office manager/administrative assistant.

I was not always in business, either. I began as a journalist as I was earning money to study to be a teacher and I was forced to get into business when teaching jobs became unavailable. Then I got another degree in counseling and guidance when I saw my students could get a degree but had no clue as to how to get a job. I have also been a personnel counselor, a counselor for Planned Parenthood, a job counselor for The Salvation Army; a church secretary, an assistant to a polygraph examiner and a paralegal for an attorney. The best teacher I have ever known is one who did not hire me and outside of that the best supervisors I have known were the church minister, the polygrapher and the lawyer. So, having done just about everything, I can help you find a job doing anything you can qualify for with these techniques that have been helping me and my clients for years.

Let's face it, you have just been laid off for no fault of your own, maybe from the best job or career you have ever had. You deserve to feel bad. For a day or so. But your ability to restore you optimism and faith in yourself and your confidence that you *can* find a job in time to keep your home, your family and whatever is dear to you—this is the first thing you must do for success. We hear in the news how people who have lost their jobs go into depression, let themselves go—even kill themselves and their families. You can't let this happen so nip that threat in the bud.

I have a master's degree in counseling and have seen the harm that job loss can do to even the most intelligent, realistic and confident workers. You may have had a warning that layoffs were coming (in which case you should start reading this book right away) or that others in your department were losing their jobs (which can create stress) or you may just come to the company office one day to find you are no longer needed or even find a lock on the door. This is the cruelest and most irresponsible way to get the bad news. But here, at least, you can say the employer is at fault for not leveling with you and showing you the respect that all employees deserve.

So how do you handle it? There is a day for "woe is me" and sharing your fears with you family, friends or a stranger at the neighborhood bar. Now, at least, you have plenty of company and this is not as hard as during better times when you might have to admit that the fault was yours, for poor performance or attitude. And your family, friends or strangers at the bar have either lost jobs themselves or know someone who has. There is a lot of sympathy to go around so lean on someone if you must and get over it.

Here I have made all the mistakes, including depression, being too proud to share the news with my friends and family, trying to go it alone without even bothering to sign up with my employment office, and going on an endless "vacation" so that I would have time to "recover from my loss." This was during good times when jobs were more plentiful and it led to a prolonged job search and acceptance of a job I really didn't like. I might have liked it if I hunted with the right attitude but an attitude that a job is "a necessary evil" leads to just that.

So if you are feeling down and need some time to recover, give yourself a day. Yes, a day to enjoy the luxury of being free, do something you have always wanted to, treat yourself to a day at the beach, a movie, a family outing or just a day of peaceful meditation. You do have a day but not much longer. This book is based on finding a job in a month and your certainly don't have a week or so to "get over it." This is your time for prayer, meditation, and visualization of the job you really want, letting off steam or whatever else may be necessary to restore you to your usual self, a positive, confident person looking forward to starting a good job in a month. In line with that schedule, you should do this in a day. Keep to your schedule and your job hunting will work for you!

GET STARTED NOW!

Now means NOW!

First, register for unemployment insurance at your local employment office. This is something too many put off, losing benefits and waiting until these offices, already busy and overburdened, are more and more difficult to reach. Some are still taking applications in person, but others will allow you to take the initial steps at least on the phone or over the Internet. Choose your method but make it a point to register this first day because you want to receive unemployment benefits as soon as possible. Don't let pride or overconfidence lead you to put if off until "tomorrow." And be sure you have your last employer's name, address and phone number and that you tell the truth about why you lost your job. For most, it is "laid off" which should qualify you for benefits, but don't lie if you lost your job for other reasons. If you lost your job because you were habitually late, because of insubordination or any other reason that might look as if job loss were your fault, clear it up with your last employer and present this in its best light because the employment office will contact that employer and lying at this point could cost you unemployment benefits, now about half of your net salary, something you need to get through the job search.

Then, read this book. Not necessarily all of it at one sitting but the first few chapters which are needed to get started. Don't try to do this during your day to get over it, your day off which you will need for yourself as the job hunt wears on. And read it until you are in the right frame of mind to be positive and forge ahead effectively and confidently for that job you want.

Next, after your day of personal assessment and contemplation, carefully assess the bottom line of what you need to earn in a month, list your job skills and come up with a list of job titles that may offer this to you. Yesterday's "secretaries" are now often "administrative assistants," "janitors" are now "custodians," "lawyers" are now "attorneys" and "job hunters" are "applicants." Use the current terminology but never forget you are a "job hunter."

You are looking for a "job," not a "career", and don't necessarily expect to match the salary or benefits of the job you just lost. After all, you may have been working up to that for years and today's job climate does not allow one to be "choosy." You may do as well or better than your last job but that will be a bonus, not a given. Be ready to apply and pursue every job for which you are qualified, and which pays enough to cover your needs, including those which offer on-the-job training. Be ready to switch fields of work or even leave a "professional" job for a business or other job that pays what you need, offers immediate work and for which you are qualified. You may find other assets like an exciting boss, friendly co-workers and a more stable job than the one you just left.

Then, get out your calendar and write "new job" one month from today. That is your prize and should motivate you to do all that is necessary to attain that goal. Promise yourself a modest "celebration" when that goal is reached. Then schedule yourself to look for a job for a full day, every work day, no matter what. That means up, dressed and ready to "work" by 9 a.m. and don't stop until 5 p.m. for most job hunters since personnel offices are open at that time, even for blue collar and labor employees. But of course you can make room for job fairs, on-site interviews or weekend or evening work if that is what you are looking for. Schedule each day with hourly blanks for activities as they occur during this month (a new "daily planner" calendar is best for this). Clear your calendar of all non-essential events during this month—you may still want to go to the doctor or dentist but you don't have time to socialize at lunch with your friends. And keep the scheduled events during this month to a minimum, a routine doctor or dental visit may be postponed for a month but not one in answer to emergency pain or troubling symptoms. You don't want to work sick and you can't be an effective job hunter while in pain.

Start out with a clear calendar except for marking the beginning of your job search, the halfway point two weeks later and acceptance of a job two weeks after that. Don't work nights and weekends (or beyond your normal work week). Overwork makes you a bad applicant and you soon will be stressed out and that will show in every application and every interview. Work "full time" even if you are only seeking a part-time job. Today's job market requires full-time effort and if you find a job in half the time, so much the better.

Treat yourself to something you like to do every day in your off time—have supper with friends, see a movie, watch television, read a good book, go to a club meeting, or spend time with your family. But don't accept invitations during your "work hours." After all, if you were working, you couldn't do these things and now you are "working at working." Keep your calendar posted where you will see it, by your telephone or work station. Check it daily so you don't miss a job activity, interview or first day of work. Next, write your resume and fill out a blank job application form. This can be done in the first day of your job hunting month. If you don't know how to write a resume, get help from the Internet where forms are posted or from the employment office. As a last resort hire someone to produce one for you same day but employers prefer applicants who are literate enough to write their own. I can't count the number of interviews I have gotten because I had a good resume and could truthfully claim it as my own. The same goes for application blanks which are the stuff of most first contacts with employers. For those who can't do this I will show you how in the next chapter. Now actually write down, hour by hour, each day's job schedule on your calendar with interviews and other appointments as they occur and with enough activity to keep you busy for every day of the month.

My job hunting schedule for office jobs looked like this:

7:a.m.—Wake up, breakfast, dress for interviews (even if I wasn't planning on going on one because hopefully I would get one.) You need to have this routine if you hope to keep it up on the job. And take care of your wardrobe, grooming, etc. before you leave the house).

8:30 a.m.—Carefully check job openings on the Internet, newspapers, television and other sources daily. This is very important and do it every day. You can't get a job if you don't know where to look for it and no one is magically going to call up wondering if you are looking for a job.
9:a.m.—Contact the companies with jobs you can qualify for. Many will not list a salary at this point but will before the interview or other decision point. Today the Internet often lists the most jobs and allows you to move the quickest. If you don't have the Internet or know how to use it, visit your library, employment office or community center which will have one and help you to use it. This is not the time to invest or wait

to install a new computer. But use the Internet from the first as it is today's best and fastest source of new jobs.

12 Noon—Lunch, at home or wherever you happen to be. Of course this time may vary if you are interviewing or tied up at the employment office, but eat lunch every day. You need to keep up your health and a hungry job hunter is a stressed job hunter and no one wants an employee who is not ready to do his best. And be sure you phone has an answering system. Interview invitations might come in while you are away from home and you don't want to miss them. A cell phone is helpful but not necessary if you have an answering machine and now is not the time to purchase a cell phone and take the time and money necessary to set it up. If you do have a cell phone, be sure to silence it while in interviews, there's nothing more embarrassing than having one employer calling you while you are talking to another.

1 p.m.—Hit the road. Afternoons are a good time to visit the job training program at your local employment office, check the Internet outside your home if you need to, visit the library for newspapers or other employment listings you do not have, visit job fairs, prospective job sites or, of course, interview if you can. If you are not otherwise busy, deliver your resume in person to companies you are most interested in. There is no substitute for finding your way to a job site, seeing what it is like, getting the

"mood" of the place and meeting at least the receptionist who will accept your application and/or resume. Some companies will indicate "no phone calls" but few will say "no visitors" since most applicants are not forward looking enough to visit. You may be lucky enough to get to meet the personnel or human resources director or even your prospective supervisor. Don't count on it but be ready to "go with the flow" if such an opportunity arises.

4 p.m. — If you have no other important business away, return home to check for responses to your contacts with employers by phone or Internet. Stay near your phone as more interview invitations are offered between 4 and 5 p.m. than at any other time of day. This time can also be used to re-contact employers you expect to hear from but don't "bug" them by contacting them twice a day. Take advantage of this "home time" to read the rest of this book, practice your resume writing and Internet skills and assess your progress of the day. Check your calendar to see that you have kept all your appointments and commitments for the day. Write, in a word or so on your calendar, how well the day went—"great," "need more contacts," "need more interviews" "job offered" or, of course, "job accepted."
5 p.m.—Leave the job search behind, watch the evening news for news of job opening announcements, job fairs or just to "stay connected"

so you have things to talk about in your interviews, spend time with friends and family, this is "your time."

The whole point of this schedule is to get you working full time at finding a job NOW. And if you do, you will have that job on schedule a month from now.

ACE THE APPLICATION BLANK

Here we come to nitty gritty job of preparing an application blank and resume. You need to do this before contacting employers on the Internet, the newspaper, the job fair or wherever you apply. Too often applicants rush to apply without evaluating themselves and their skills, only to be passed over in the early stages because they don't sound grounded in themselves or, even worse, after working hard for an interview because they just don't know what they are really good at, can't offer related past experience or can't give the phone number of a previous employer. Be prepared from the first with an application blank filled out and a resume (both of which you carry with you for your reference and in case an employer just hasn't gotten yours yet). The application blank and the resume are really two different versions of the same information, with the resume being a little longer and more detailed. But your process in preparing them is basically the same. Be sure you have at hand a complete list of your jobs, company addresses and phone numbers, job skills, education and references which you have contacted and asked for a recommendation for a job you are seeking.

This is an absolute must. Don't try to "wing it" by assuming that a previous employer will remember you, let alone have something good to say about you when called out of the blue from a prospective employer. And do this for every job you have had for the past 10 years, accounting for all time unemployed and beginning with your last job. Even if you were unemployed to do job training, take care of children at home, travel or live abroad, or just a long job search, indicate this on your resume. Employers are suspicious about long periods of unaccounted time—did you take a "long vacation" or, heaven forbid, were you in jail, writing a book or whatever? Whatever it is, account for it in your resume and if it's something like jail time, indicate you would like to discuss that in your interview and be prepared to explain why, in spite of that, you would be a good employee.

The Internet has application forms you can print out, so does the library and many companies hand them out in their personnel offices or at job fairs. Type them; most handwriting is not legible and you want your prospective employer at least to be able to read it. You can't expect a company to hire you if they can't read your application. Here is a typical fictitious application blank (All information is strictly fictional)

ABC Enterprises
123 Fourth St.
New Job, California 94066

Name: Suzy Job Hunter
Address: 1070 Enterprise Ave., Job Capitol, CA 94077
Home Phone Number: (650) 777-1111
Business Phone Number: None
e-mail: suzyjobhunter@yahoo.com
Date: Today's date

JOB SKILLS
Five years of administrative assistant experience in sales, human
resources and public relations settings

Working knowledge of Word Perfect 200, Excel, Power Point,
Internet and web site creation and management

Customer service in person and on the phone and Internet
Supervision of 10 department employees
Human Resources, conduct of hiring interviews, administration
of employee benefits

EMPLOYMENT HISTORY
Position: Administrative Assistant
Company Name: XYZ Company
Company Address: 345 Lost Job Avenue, Silicon Valley, CA
94077
Company e-mail: lostjob@yahoo.com
Supervisor's Name and Title: Tom Jones, Personnel Director

Dates Employed (month and year) January 1, 2006 to January 1,
2009

Reason for Leaving: Laid off because of company financial problems

(Repeat this as often as they have blanks)
Employment Application Blank, Page Two

EDUCATION
School/College: Community College of San Mateo
Address: 300 Skyline Boulevard, San Mateo, CA 94066
Phone Number: (650) 666-9999
Major Course of Study or Degree: B.A. in Business Administration

PERSONAL
Are you a United States citizen or legal immigrant? Yes, a citizen
If not, why? N/A
Condition of Health: Excellent
Do you have any disabilities that might interfere with your work? None

Have you ever been convicted of a crime? No
Have you ever been dismissed from a job? No
Have you ever served in the military? No
Days lost to illness in the past year? Two

List friends or relatives employed here: None
Are you willing to relocate or travel? Yes
List activities and leisure interests (do not list any that indicate race, religion or political party): Chairperson for Job Center community chorus, center on local women's basketball league, Skyridge bridge club, reading fiction and poetry

Why do you want to work for ABC Enterprises? I know your reputation for fine quality service and professional management, your office is close to my home, I have

experience and skills for your Community Relations
Department opening and I had occasion to visit your offices
a year ago when posting flyers for our basketball
tournament.

LET'S LOOK AT IT

Of course, your application will be different for
everything after the first block with name, address,
etc. Be specific in listing job skills, if you have worked
with office or construction equipment, name the
system or equipment as many employers look here
first for quick hires. List supervisory experience at any
level, job foreman, department head or assistant,
sales manager, etc. Give this your best attention and
carry a "dummy" application blank with you so you will
not have to start fresh with every one you fill out. For
dates employed, give month and year. If there is a
break between jobs, explain here "January 2004-
2006, full-time college student" or whatever. For
"Reason for Leaving" say "Laid off" or any other
readily understandable reason. If not, say "will
discuss in interview." You should keep sensitive
information off the routine application blank and be
prepared to discuss this in the interview.

If you were in jail, for instance, and you are
asked about this in the interview, be ready to look

your interviewer squarely in the face and say you were in jail a year for whatever reason but that you have done your time and, after all, an average in one in every hundred people in the United States has been in jail at some time. Here you can give your parole officer or another recommendation, who has been contacted in the same way you would a previous employer, and hope you have an understanding employer. Better to do this up front because lying about this or anything else on your application blank is cause for dismissal.

For Education, give whatever you have. College is fine but a trade school is just what a building contractor or bridge builder is looking for so put this in the same form as you would a college. List high school and diploma which is enough for many entry level positions. Community colleges are generally as acceptable as four-year colleges for everything short of professional jobs and there are excellent art academies, cooking and bar tending schools and adult education courses that you can list. If you only went to high school, list this by name—Sky View High School, etc. and if you have a high school equivalency certificate, list that. Don't let a lack of formal education stop you, most employers are more interested in job experience, anyway.

For Personal, beware of any questions that indicate whether your sexual preference, marital status, number of children, husband's name or occupation, race or national origin, or other things protected by the U.S. Constitution. An exception here is "The Salvation Army" which is not a church here but a welfare organization and part of your experience. If there are spaces for discriminatory things, simply indicate "N/A," not applicable. Any company that discriminates against you on these bases is violating the law and you probably don't want to work for this company, anyway,

Be careful not to indicate these things in listing your activities. If you are in the Sacred Heart Church Choir, for instance, say church choir. If you are a volunteer for a political party, say community volunteer. Don't open yourself to any possible discrimination by being the one to mention these things.

Give special thought to why you want to work for the company. You should have the skills and experience for the job and say so. Beyond that try to personalize your application by offering a reason why you , rather than all the others applying for this job, want to work for them. Here you should look up the company on the Internet, look at ads in magazines, newspapers and television, comment on a pleasant experience as their customer, your admiration of their products, be honest but positive and individual as possible. This is the last item on the application blank and it is the last impression you leave as an applicant.

MASTER YOUR RESUME

Unlike the application blank, the resume is a product of your own creation and you have time to design one that will show you off at your best. It will have basically the same information as on your resume but you are in charge of choosing the order of information, what information you wish to present and in what format. It should be neatly created on plain white paper (no fancy colors or expensive finishes) with a word processor which you have or which you can use at your library, community center or adult education center. These places often have people to help you use the machine but what you say and how you say it is your job. As a last resort, hire someone or get a friend to prepare one for you if you can't do this in a day but say in the interview, if asked, that it is your personal resume rather than you prepared it. Here is a resume for Suzy Job Hunter who signed the application in the last chapter:

RESUME
Suzy Job Hunter
1070 Enterprise Ave.
Job Capitol, CA 94077
(650) 777-1111
suzyjobhunter@yahoo.com

Applying for: Position in human resources, public relations or advertising departments.

JOB SKILLS
Five years experience with Word Perfect 2000, Excel, Power Point, Internet web site creation and management, supervision of 10 employees, administration of health and other employee benefits, conduct of employment interviews

EMPLOYMENT HISTORY
Assistant to Human Reserves Director, XYZ Company
345 Lost Job Avenue
Silicon Valley, CA 94077
 Phone –(408) 658-1000, e-mail—
xyzcompany@yahoo.com
Supervisor-Tom Jones
In this position as Mr. Jones' Assistant, I handled his personal phone calls, reception and inter-departmental meetings within this personnel search company, helped to conduct employment interviews, evaluation and follow-up; posted openings on company Internet site, supervised 10 other employees in our department and managed health and other employee benefits

I left because the company has downsized due to the current difficult financial climate. Mr. Jones will be happy to give you a recommendation for me and I am enclosing his written recommendation.

(Repeat this for each job you have.)

EDUCATION

Terra Nova High School,
3600 Terra Nova Boulevard
Pacifica, CA 94044
Phone—(650) 123-2457
E-Mail—terranovahigh@hotmail.com

I was graduated in June, 2000 with a courses in Business and Psychology and a grade point average of 3..5 on a 4.0 scale. I was captain of the women's basketball team, a soprano in our high school chorus, a member of the newspaper and yearbook staff s, and voted "most congenial" by my senior class.

Community College of San Mateo
300 Skyline Boulevard
San Mateo, CA 94066
Phone---(650) 666-9999
E-Mail---skylinecollege@yahoo.com

I was graduated in June, 2004 with a major in Business Administration and a minor in Counseling and a grade point average of 3.3 on a 4.0 scale. I was a center on the women's basketball team, a soprano in our college chorus, editor of our creative writing magazine, and participated in helping the Salvation Army food bank in our community service project. My faculty sponsor was Sally Mason and she can be reached in the high school business department.

REFERENCES

Tom Jones, Personnel Director
XYZ Company
345 Lost Job Avenue
Silicon Valley, CA 94077
Phone –(650) 666-9999
E-Mail—xyzcompany@ayhoo.com

Sally Mason, Business Instructor
Skyline College
300 Skyline Boulevard
San Mateo, CA 94066
Phone---(650) 666-9999
E-Mail---skylinecollege@yahoo.com

Mary Ann Superwoman
The Salvation Army
1230 San Mateo Boulevard
San Mateo, CA 94006
(650) 244-1658
E-Mail—salvationarmy@hotmail.com

PERSONAL

I am single with no family obligations that could interfere
with my work schedule. In my spare time I sing in our
local community chorus, play in the Job Capitol Basketball
team, play bridge at the community center and do creative
writing when I can, now I'm getting together my first book
of poems.

I am interested in working with you at ABC Enterprises because I know of your fine reputation for high quality computer education and service, I live near your office so it will be an easy commute, I especially am interested in your Community Relations Department because of my media and personnel experience and having been laid off a week ago, I am fresh and ready to go back to work. I had a very pleasant experience delivering a basketball flyer for your employee sports program with your receptionist who was very friendly and even offered me a cup of coffee as I waited for my flyer to b e approved for posting.
I would like the opportunity to meet you and talk about your position and am looking forward to hearing from you.

LET'S LOOK AT IT

Basically this is the same information as you have on your resume, only presented more fully with recommendations and in a way that is best for you. Here mention the specific opening as well as others you qualify for. The company may have more than one and you want to be considered for anything in your field that may come up.

Your job skills are still the thing most employers are looking for as well as your job history, accounting for every lapse in employment. Go back five jobs if you have them as far as 10 years (this is an important indicator of stability).

For "Education" go back to high school even if you have a college associate or four-year degree and include your grade point average if it is a 3.0 or better on a 4.0 point scale. To give a fuller picture of yourself and mention the teacher who knows you best as a possible reference. Be sure you have this teacher's current address and phone and call him just as you would a reference to let him know you are looking for a job. (Some applicants think this is silly but if teachers like to be remembered in a positive way by their students).

If you have two college degrees or diplomas from trade schools, or if you have been away from high school for more than 10 years, this may not be necessary. But for applicants in blue collar, trade or service jobs, this could help give you a fuller resume.)

Don't make your resume too long. Two or three pages at most. After all, you don't want this employer to have to spend too much time reading before he calls you for an interview.

References are not usually requested on an application blank but should be included in your resume to pave the way to a quick interview. Have a letter of reference from your last employer if possible. Some employers call your references before asking for an interview but in this financial crisis, your references are solid and you really don't care if they call them first. Be sure that all past supervisors listed here are willing to recommend you, rather than just give the dates of your employment which they are ethically obligated to do, and list those who are good on the phone, not dull and disinterested. Your past supervisors will be contacted anyway so save this for the best ones, the ones that will rave about you. And be sure that any personal references like the Salvation Army are willing to accept this additional responsibility for your activities and will say some good things about you. If they are lukewarm or not really interested in recommending you, move on to your next potential reference. Most companies limit their search to three references, if they want more they will ask. This is, for many, the most important part of the resume—they want to know firsthand, usually on the phone, what people really think about you so give this section your best effort.

In "Personal" you can venture information that you may not want to offer on a resume, like being single with no family responsibilities. It is one thing to for them to ask this, which could be a kind of discrimination against married applicants with families, and another if you choose to offer it. Still you should NOT offer information about race, marital status, religion, political party or anything else that could lead to discrimination on the part of the hiring company. The same applies to your activities, it is a "community chorus" rather than the "St. Andrew's Presbyterian Church chorus" or even "church" chorus, which will lead to the question of which church chorus you sing in. You might feel comfortable about answering this in the interview, but keep it out of your resume. Your work at the Salvation Army is understood to be a welfare organization, not a church membership.

Repeat and perhaps elaborate on why you are interested in working at ABC Company (this information will be different for each company and some applicants omit it because it will cause you to write something different for every company you apply to. But it's a simple "copy and paste" on your word processor and it's impressive if you have a special reason for wanting to work for them.) If you don't have a clue why you want to work for them, save it for the interview and have an answer for this by that time. Some companies, especially when they have many applicants to choose from, are more interested in this than any part of the resume.

ASK FOR AN INTERVIEW! Usually it's more friendly to say you would like to meet them than to get an interview, but it's the same thing. You must meet them before they will offer you a job and you surely don't want to work for someone who refuses, or doesn't bother, to meet you. One of the leading reasons an employee looses his job early on is that he just doesn't like the people he works with or they just don't like him. Get over this hurdle and don't accept a job before you interview.

Have a copy of your application and copies of your resume with you at home and take them with you as you go out to the Employment Office, to deliver to employers personally when you can and to take to the interview. Even if the company has a copy of it already, carry them with you in case there is more than one interviewer or if a busy employer has mislaid it. This happened to me once and the fact that I had another ready copy for them facilitated the interview and helped me get the job.

WHAT IF YOU ARE "JOE THE PLUMBER'?

You have the same routine as "Suzy Job Hunter," "Sam the Salesman," or "Peter Professional" and job hunters in any other field. You will probably have a less lengthy resume as Joe the Plumber but you should write one from the application blank that almost all trade industries require. You may also find more openings, thanks to all the construction jobs being opened up by government. Your job hunting schedule may vary according to your usual work schedule but hiring offices, your first contact, are usually open during the normal business day. You need the same discipline of filing for employment benefits the first day, reading this book and working full time at finding a job. You will have to use the

Internet as most jobs are posted there, but a trip to the library or Employment office will take care of this. Job losses are occurring across the board in all kinds of work and new government jobs, also will come in all fields. For every plumber hired, there is an office support staff and, a sales force to sell his company's work. So join the crew, we are all in the same boat!

MAKE CONTACT...

Now for the important step of applying for jobs on the Internet, in newspapers, on television, by help wanted signs and word of mouth. Because one of these WILL be your next employer and no employer is magically going to call you out of the blue, wondering if you need a job. This, and following up on every contact, should be part of your daily routine because it will lead to the job you are seeking.

THE INTERNET

These days with a time intensive schedule and the many jobs out there, working with the Internet is the first priority of many job hunters. Again, this is not the time to invest in a computer, wait for it to be installed and take a full course on using it. If you don't have a computer or know how to use it, go to a friend, your state employment office, library or community center who will have equipment and show you how to use it. Once you get started, the process is repetitive and you will learn quickly.

The most helpful sites for jobs are Monster Jobs and Hot Jobs, which you will find by entering the "jobs" on the search engine on the first page of your screen. These will tell you about literally hundreds of jobs in all fields throughout the United States and overseas. On a month's schedule, you will probably want to look close to home so cue in your hometown and/or the nearest metropolitan center and the kind of work you are looking for. It can be "sales," "business" or a specific trade like "plumber."

On Monster, you will be immediately given information on the many jobs in the category you have requested with information about location, skills and experience required and other information you need, often omitting company name and salary which will be given to you later. On Hot Mail, you must sign in and wait for the appropriate jobs to be e-mailed to you. In either case, the Internet is your contact with these openings and you must check it daily for more job information, screening, and possible interviews at the job site. These two computer sites have openings for blue collar, white collar and professional jobs all in one place and the process of contacting companies on the Internet is the same for all.

Have an application blank with you so you can readily recall information about your job skills, past employers, etc. After application information is cued in, the form will say "apply" or "submit" Here Joe the Plumber may have a shorter form with less to say but with the new government jobs in construction, he may have more openings than Suzy Job Hunter, Sam the Salesman or Peter Professional. And the government with its new job stimulus plan now is the source of most sources so cue in "government jobs" where indicated. You will be contacted about openings for which you qualify and you can take it from there as indicated by the employer.

GOVERNMENT JOBS

Now the best source of new jobs, the government is listing jobs on its own web site (usually your hometown, county, state or U.S. gov.).They also advertise in local newspapers and television stations for jobs ready for immediate hire. It is to the government's advantage to fill these jobs quickly and this plays into your hand as a job hunter. They usually indicate salary, benefits, location and other vital information immediately to expedite the hiring process. For once here is an employer ready to hire as you are to work. Check these listings and follow up every day.

Many government jobs will be only for a year or so (the popular estimate of the duration of this recession) but by then you will be on your financial feet again and some may lead to permanent work, with the government or with private companies with good employee and health benefits. Also you are a "civil servant" and have protection against discrimination and unjustified dismissal

COMPANY LISTINGS

Many large companies list their openings on their own Internet job sites or on listings on a bulletin board in the company offices. This favors their own employees seeking to move up in the company or visitors who may already know about their company and have reason to want to work there. Check these out on the Internet and when applying for jobs on their premises because they could be express routes to an interview and a quick acceptance of your new job. You will know about the job, be aware of the job site and actually be in the same place where an interview would take place. Don't be afraid to ask about the job in the company personnel or human resources department and apply for it while there, if only to leave a copy of your resume which many companies will accept in instead of making you fill out an application while there. You may actually get a screening interview in that office or on a rare occasion for a job they must fill immediately, an interview with your prospective supervisor.

ADS IN NEWSPAPERS AND OTHER PUBLICATIONS

Ads in your local newspaper, once the first place to look for jobs, have suffered with the newspapers themselves in this recession. When I checked my hometown of Pacifica near San Francisco, I found only two job openings and in San Francisco there was less than a page where there used to be a whole section. But these jobs at least al all in your local area and some will list a phone number to contact an employer, rather than just an e-mail address repose where you must wait for Monster or Hot Jobs to contact you. This is a gold mine, a straight line to the interview! So check these ads and ads in professional journals or other publications that list jobs daily.

If there is a phone number listed, be prepared by having your application blank by your side, give some thought as to what you will say on the phone, relax and give it your best. And read the next chapter about interviews first since answering an ad on the phone IS an interview.

"HELP WANTED" SIGNS AND "WORD OF MOUTH"

Some small businesses still post "help wanted" signs in the window instead of waiting or paying the fee necessary to advertise on the Internet or a newspaper. These jobs may be close to your home and almost guarantee you a chance for an immediate interview with someone in charge. These are often for minimum wage jobs or part-time work but they can assure you of a job close to home, even within walking distance, and what is usually a streamlined hiring process.

If you are interested in the job, go in and say you would like to apply for it, resume in hand as these businesses often do not have application blanks of their own and need the information quickly and clearly typed for quick reference. Give this the same thought as a scheduled interview, read the next section on interviews, be sure you are well groomed and dressed appropriately (or you shouldn't be there) and be ready for an interview that could lead to a job offer from your prospective employer.

If you have a friend or family member in a company with a job opening, their "word of mouth" may be your lead to a job. If this job is advertised on the Internet or newspaper, follow the usual route of application. If it is "secret" information, known only to those inside the company, don't rush out and just apply for it, giving away your friend or family member as the source and getting out of step with the employment process. But if it is a hot job your really want, there is no harm in stopping by the company site and asking if they might be needing a salesman, administrative assistant or whatever the job is. They may just say that all openings pass through regular channels and to watch for it on the Internet, but you have met the receptionist at least and gotten a feel for the company. In the case of a job opening that is really "open," you can mention that you heard about it from a friend or employee and this often leads to an inside track to hiring.

So really "milk" all of these sources of job openings daily and follow through as your first active step to finding your next job.

INTERVIEW, INTERVIEW, INTERVIEW

Now for the all-important interview. This is the "magic moment" when you meet your prospective supervisor and others in the company and where you must make the impression necessary for them to hire you. And this is also you chance to size them up, ask any questions you may have about salary, benefits and "when would you like me to start?" Or simply "Let's stay in touch" if decision has been not reached or "It was good to meet you" if you don't think you want the job but just want to thank them for talking with you. Don't say, "thank you for your time" (how unexciting) and beware if that's all they have to say to you.

This is your dress rehearsal for a job so get there on time, dress appropriately for the job and be fresh, sharp and positive. Visit the job site beforehand to see how to get there by auto, bus or whatever, how long it takes, what the company site looks like and how other people dress. You don't need to identify yourself, you can just ask if they have a company bulletin board, a cafeteria open to the public or—for a real look at them, ask to use their restroom. I would never work in a place that refuses to offer a restroom to a needy passer-by and this is one way to see if they are sensitive to their community, afraid of visitors for security reasons or simply "off limits" to the public.

Get there 15 minutes ahead of time so you can get the "feel" of the office and upon entering, identify yourself and mention the person you have an appointment for and the time of your interview so the receptionist can let them know you are there. If the receptionist is busy, don't engage in conversation, but if not or if she starts a conversation, follow along about the weather or any other safe subject. Observe the office carefully without staring and listen for the tone of voices, are they casual and friendly or stressed and overworked?

If the interviewer is 15 minutes late, you can casually ask the receptionist if he knows you are there. Another 15 minutes and you might ask again, wondering if there is some cause for the delay. Sometimes an interviewer is running late on another interview or he might be away from the office with no chance of getting to see you in any reasonable time. In the latter case, ask to reschedule your interview if you have better things to do on your month's job hunting schedule than wait around for someone who is not considerate of your time. If the company is serious about interviewing you, they will re-schedule and hopefully be on time. If not you would be spending your precious time with another, more serious interview.

However, if on entering the office you see it is not a place you can stand working in—loud industrial noise, quibbling employees, total ignoring of your presence or a receptionist totally unaware of your scheduled interview, just say "thank you, I'll be in touch," and leave. You are saving the interviewer's time as well as yours by not going through with the interview. And check your contacts with prospective employers to avoid this happening again. However, if this is a job you really want, you might chance waiting for this interviewer as long as you can on the day's schedule—maybe he honestly forgot you were coming and will be there as soon as possible or maybe he had a personal or business emergency that will allow him to get to the office in the next hour. Then wait for him, it should impress upon him that you really want the job and cared enough to wait.

Now let's listen in on an interview for Sam the Salesman at a local men's clothing store.

SAM (TO THE RECEPTIONIST)
Hello, I'm Sam the Salesman and I have an appointment to interview with Mr. Manager at 1 o'clock.

THE RECEPTIONIST
Yes, Mr. Manager is expecting you. I'll let him know you are here.

MANAGER

Hello, Sam. How are you today? Have a seat (points to a seat near his desk). We've been so busy I haven't had a chance to straighten up the office.

SAM

You do seem busy, lots of customers out there (a compliment these days)

MANAGER

Yes, we're doing well. Let's see what we have here (takes a quick look at Sam's resume which he carries inside his employment folder for reference if necessary) I see you have experience selling men's clothing at Macy's.

SAM

Yes, I was there for five years before they started laying off people. I want to work with a company that has more business like yours.

MANAGER

Yes, Black and Brown Brothers has been in business for 20 years and we cater to the economy minded customer who wants to dress well on a budget with styles not already out in the big stores. Here you can get a suit for $199 and trousers without the jacket for just $100 with a wide variety of styles and alterations included. We can make you look like a million dollars in a suit tailored to fit you, same day, with our in-house tailors standing by.

SAM

Wow, Macy's didn't do that for twice as much!

MANAGER

Exactly! That's why the Macy's down the street is out of business and we're still here. Did you know that the mayor bought a suit here last month?

SAM

No, I didn't. That's a real recommendation.

MANAGER

We use it all the time. We need someone with experience selling men's clothing who is really interested in the success of our customers. I see you are wearing a Macy's design suit today.

SAM

Yes, it's probably an expensive imitation of one of yours.

MANAGER

You know, it is. It's a lot like our "interview special"— sharp but conservative with a sports jacket in subtle contrast to the trousers. That's just what we would recommend if you got it here. (Pauses) What are your salary and commission requirements and do you need benefits?

SAM

(CAREFULLY) Well, I earned $2,000 a month plus commission at Macy's with full employee and health benefits.

MANAGER

That seems reasonable for the kind of salesman we are looking for. When can you start?

SAM

Right now, if you need me.

MANAGER

That won't be necessary but come in at 8:30 tomorrow morning so I can show you around before we open at 9. You will be working 9 to 5 on weekdays and alternating afternoon shifts for one day every other weekend. How does that sound?

SAM

That sounds great! Thank you and I'll see you at 8:30 tomorrow morning.

LET'S LOOK AT IT

This is, of course, the kind of interview both Sam and the Manager were hoping for. Sam knew the sales business and the Manager knew a good candidate when he saw one. Both were sure enough to "hire" and "accept" on the spot without delay. If they weren't sure, one or the other would say they enjoyed talking with each other and that they would stay in touch.

Let's listen in on another interview for Suzy Job Hunter that didn't go so well.

SALES DEPARTMENT HEAD

Hello, Suzy, have a seat.

SUZY

Thanks. (gushing) Oh, what a beautiful office!

SALES DEPARTMENT HEAD

It's standard for our company, we like to make a good impression. Let's see what we have here (pauses to look at resume) I see you were in the sales department of Macy's down the street.

SUZY

Yes, I was there for two years but we had to close because our customers stopped coming because of the recession.

SALES DEPARTMENT HEAD

But they are still coming here. Why do you suppose?

SUZY

I don't know, maybe because your clothes are cheaper than at Macy's.

SALES DEPARTMENT HEAD

There's nothing "cheap" about our clothes, we just give you style for less. (pauses to look again at resume). Well, how much do you need to earn?

SUZY

How about $2,000 a month plus benefits?

SALES DEPARTMENT HEAD

That's no problem, for the right person. Why do you want to work for us?

SUZY
Well, I need a job, I haven't worked for a month, and your ad said you were hiring now.

SALES DEPARTMENT MANAGER
We are interviewing now. We won't hire until next week after we have interviewed all our applicants. We have 20 people interested in this job. So it has been good talking with you and we will stay in touch.

SUZY
(Openly disappointed) Is there anything else I can tell you, I could start immediately.

SALES DEPARTMENT MANAGER
Thank you. We'll be in touch if we want you.

LET'S LOOK AT IT

Suzy was not nearly as well prepared or as well received as Sam in the same industry. Suzy gushed over the company office; perhaps too much for someone who had worked at Macy's whose company offices might have been even more plush. She gave a reason for being unemployed without being asked (a plea for sympathy over the recession which this interviewer might not want to discuss at all). She couldn't give a good reason for wanting to work at this company which was obviously more busy than Macy's and failed to take advantage of complimenting the manager on his company's business as Sam did. She called their clothing "cheap" rather than "style for less" as the manager prompted her. She asks for the same salary as Sam but fails to mention the benefits that are important to any employee. Her only reason for wanting to work for the new company is that she needs a job and misstates the ad, saying they are "hiring" now rather than "interviewing" now. And the interviewer dismisses her and her chances for a job with him with a polite "we'll stay in touch."

Now let's listen in on an interview for Peter Professional, a laid off high school English teacher, applying at Better High, a high school in the same area that needs a teacher to finish the semester for one that is having an operation.

ENGLISH DEPARTMENT CHAIRMAN
Hello, Peter. I see you were working at East High before the big layoff.

PETER
Yes, that was a real blow to a lot of us teachers. I'm just glad I saw your ad on the Internet.

DEPARTMENT CHAIRMAN
We don't usually advertise positions but one of our remedial English instructors just had surgery and we need someone next week. Have you taught remedial?

PETER

Yes, that was half my load at East High. These kids need to learn how to spell and write a sentence. It's a very rewarding class to teach.

DEPARTMENT CHAIRMAN

I wish some of our other teachers felt that way. They want to get away from the basics and teach advanced students who can share their appreciation of great writing and literature. So your load would be entirely remedial English, five classes a day, five days a week. How would you feel about that?

PETER

I would enjoy it and feel challenged to provide this to students who need it.

DEPARTMENT CHAIRMAN

Oh, ours really need it all right. Did you know we rank in the lower 25 percentile of overall language scores because our students come from working class families, many of whom speak Spanish at home? How is your Spanish?

PETER

Good. I took it as a second language and like to travel in Mexico. In fact, I have taught English as a second language in our night school.

DEPARTMENT HEAD

Bueno. Entonces, cuando puede Vd. empezar? ("Good, when can you begin?"testing Peter's Spanish)

PETER

Hoy, si es necessario. (Today if necessary)

DEPARTMENT HEAD

We don't need you today, we're covered for the rest of the week. But we do need someone next Monday. Can I call East High and check your references?

PETER

Yes, you can as well as from City Night School and the other references I give.

DEPARTMENT HEAD

I assume you have read our job description and know our salary and benefits. You would be temporary for a month with a per deim, then we would make you permanent give you a review with full salary and benefits.

PETER

That sounds good to me.

DEPARTMENT HEAD

I have two more interviews this afternoon but you sound good. Call me after four and I'll know.

PETER

Thank you. I'll do that and I would enjoy working at your school. You have a good campus and some of our students are lucky enough to end up here.

DEPARTMENT HEAD

One good thing is that our student-teacher ratio is less that at East High, thanks to fund raising activities of the students and teachers themselves which have given us some job security in these tough times. Call me this afternoon at four.

LET'S LOOK AT IT

Peter did well on this interview because he got to the right place at the right time and had experience in the particular class needed in another high school in the area. He showed expertise and an honest interest in working with remedial students (something most other teachers don't like) and he even had experience at City Night School giving him even more experience in this class. He spoke Spanish and could converse with his interviewer, giving him valuable experience in teaching English to students who spoke Spanish at home. He was ready to teach immediately if needed and gave a reason why he would like to teach at Better High where job security is better than the school he left. The Department head leveled with him that he is interviewing other candidates but his invitation to check back with him at a certain time assures Peter that he has a real chance at this job.

All successful interviews have a few things in common besides the usual arriving on time and dressed for the occasion. They follow the lead of the interviewer, answer all questions directly and thoughtfully, show an honest eagerness to work in this particular place and are ready to work on short notice and with the salary, benefits and duties indicated. They are honest, not gushing, and show preparation ahead of time on the crucial questions of why the applicant wants to work for this particular company and why he, of all people, is particularly suited to the job.

It's good to practice an interview with a job coach at the state employment office, a fellow applicant, or a family member to be sure you are ready for this big moment in the job hunting process. Because a good interview is the most important step in getting a job and if you do interview well consistently, you WILL have a new job in a month.

REAL INTERVIWS

     Until now all information on the application blank and resume has been fictional, but now I would like to share some REAL interviews from the Suzy Job Hunter stage of my job hunting career. There were really "magical moments" from my interviews with the minister, polygrapher and lawyer I mentioned in the Introduction. Because here is not only the key to getting a job, but to getting a job with someone you would really like to work with.

THE MINISTERS
(Note here there are two ministers involved, Junior Minister and Senior Minister.)

JUNIOR MINISTER
Hello, Suzy, how are you today?

SUZY
I'm fine. I say your ad for a secretary so I want to apply for the job.

JUNIOR MINISTER
And we need a secretary, frankly I'm getting tired of the job and I want to give it to someone else.

SUZIE
That's me.

JUNIOR MINISTER
(glancing at my resume)—So you worked for the Salvation Army.

SUZIE

Yes, in Denver.

JUNIOR MINISTER

They are a good bunch, the Army. My dad was one.
Well, we are grateful for your experience. When can
you start?

SUZY

The job, you mean?

JUNIOR MINISTER

(with some authority) Yes, the job.

SUZY

How about Monday?

JUNIOR MINISTER

Monday it is. And the salary is in the paper, $10 an
hour, half time."

SUZY

Perfect.

JUNIOR MINISTER

(closing the deal) Perfect!
At this point the SENIOR MINISTER comes in Hi,
Tom. Sorry to be late, traffic is awful out there.
(Looking at Suzy) So this is Suzy.

JUNIOR MINISTER

(officially)--Yes, Jim. This is Suzy Job Hunter, our new
secretary.

(At this moment all three of us froze, realizing that the Junior Minister had just"hired" me without consulting his superior. What would Jim do?)

SENIOR MINISTER

(With a quick smile, looking me straight in the face and shaking my hand warmly)—Welcome to our Church!

This was perhaps the most "magic" moment I have ever had in an interview. I was hired by a Senior Minister strong enough to want to put his seal of approval on my hire and kind enough not to step on his errant Junior Minister in the process. Needless to say, my first duty was to have lunch with them so they could get to know the person they just hired. The Senior Minister accepted me and my grandson into the church and performed a rededication ceremony for my marriage. Now, 30 years later, I am still a member of that church.

THE POLYGRAPHER

(He studied my resume a full 15 minutes before coming out of his inner office to greet me.)—Hello, I'm Thomas Johnson.

SUZY

I'm Suzy Job Hunter.

POLYGRAPHER

Won't you come in. (leading the way to his inner office). Well, so you want to work in polygraph. Do you know what that is?

SUZY

You're a lie detector.

POLYGRAPHER

Well, not exactly but that's what most people think. We do give tests to see if we can detect if a person is telling the truth or not. Sometimes we don't know and we say those tests are inconclusive. Does this interfere with any of your personal beliefs?

SUZY

No.

POLYGRAPHER

(Without looking at my resume which he knows by heart) So you have some good secretarial experience—with a minister. Ministers don't lie, do they?

SUZY

Not that one, anyway.

POLYGRAPHER

Most of what you will do is reports, like this (pulling one off his desk). Can you do this from a dictaphone?

SUZY

(taking time to look at it). Yes, I did these for personnel in The Salvation Army.

POLYGRAPHER

I warn you, I'm a perfectionist when it comes to my commas and semi colons.

SUZY

No problem, I taught Freshman English at one time.

POLYGRAPHER

Good. But I usually dictate them with the report. But you have to catch me if I'm wrong. (examines at her through his glasses). You will be hearing from us at the end of the week.

SUZY

I'd like to tell you more about my other experience—

POLYGRAPHER

(Smiling) You did just fine, Suzy. You will be hearing from us the end of the week. (With a pause that indicated the interview was over in less than 5 minutes)

SUZY

Well, thank you. It was good talking with you.

POLYGRAPHER

Likewise. My wife will call you on Friday.

He did not need to go over my resume at the interview because he had already taken it in and he had a short interview because his time was expensive and he was an expert at sizing up people. He decided if my references checked out, he would hire me. And he did, his wife called me Friday afternoon and I began the next Monday. He was a gentleman of the old school and always "Mr. Johnson" to me. But he and his wife became dear friends and he gave me the use of an office he didn't need plus equipment to write my first book, which is dedicated to them. When he retired, my husband and I gave him a "retirement dinner" which he said "he would always remember." And his positive recommendation helped me get my next job with the lawyer.

THE LAWYER
(Coming in a half hour late for the interview after phoning his receptionist that he was "running late but to hold me" if she could. Since this was a good job in my hometown and I was not scheduled elsewhere, I waited)
I'm sorry to be late, I got tied up in a game of golf. Do you play golf?

SUZY
No, but my husband does.

LAWYER
Really, what course?

SUZY

The one here in town.

LAWYER

Well, if I were here in town, I would have been on time. I was at the public course in the city. (pauses and looks right at Suzy) Why would you like to work for a lawyer?

SUZY

A good lawyer can help people.

LAWYER

And what about a bad lawyer?

SUZY

I don't want to work with a bad lawyer.

LAWYER

(smiling) Well, you're safe with me. I'm a good lawyer. (pauses) So you saw the salary and hours in the ad in the paper?

SUZY

Yes, I did.

LAWYER

I had my receptionist check out your references and you're clean. I guess ministers and polygraphers don't lie.

SUZY

Not the ones I worked for.

LAWYER

And you only work for the good ones, like good lawyers. Can you start Monday?

SUZY

Yes, I can. But just one thing—why did you hire me, I don't have any legal experience.

LAWYER

I hired you precisely because you don't have legal experience and know nothing about the law. That way you will believe everything I tell you. And I need a secretary that believes everything I tell her. So I'll see you Monday at 9.

SUZY

Monday at 9. Thank you.

This lawyer took his receptionist and me to lunch often, brought us tulips at Easter and poinsettias at Christmas and when he needed to break the news to us that he would be retiring, he took us out for drinks at the neighborhood bar so we could digest the sad news. He gave us glowing recommendations to other lawyers who hired us immediately and we gave him a retirement party at Mary's home. I still have lunch with him now and then whenever I need some free legal advice.

"Magic Moments"

So when were the "magic moments" in each of these interviews? With the Senior Minister, it was when he quickly digested the fact that his subordinate had jumped the gun to hire me and took charge by officially welcoming me to the church. With the polygrapher, it was when I could confidently say I could type the report and was wise enough to stop short of making him listen to my other experience, which he had on my resume. With the attorney, it was that waited for him, I had no legal experience and expressed my concern for working with a "good" employer.

It is also interesting to chart the pace and level of trust in these interviews. The total interview at the church lasted longest since I was actually interviewed by two people. The senior minister hired me on a sheer leap of faith—he trusted the judgment of the junior minister and figured he'd get to know me soon enough, any. The polygrapher trusted me as far as he could go in an interview and only waited to check my references before hiring me. The lawyer checked my references in advance and knew after hearing that I had no preconceptions about the law and wanted to work for a "good" lawyer which he was, that he would hire me.

All three of these interviews succeeded because we were willing to go "outside the box" in the interview. The minister was late and so was the lawyer. The polygrapher hardly broke a smile until the end when he had already decided on me and wanted to soften what I perceived as a lost interview. If I had been upset that a junior minister was the one to hire me, or needed lots of smiles to assure me that I was "winning" or walked out because the lawyer was late on the golf course, I would have lost those jobs. And these turned out to be some of the best people I have ever worked with.

Analyze your interviews and see if any of these "magic moments" happened and if you failed to cash in on them. Anything short of flirting personally with you, suggesting something unethical or illegal, and acting in a way that you know you don't want to work with this person, is okay. Give it a chance and see if this can also be a "magic interview" for you as well.

IT'S HALF TIME

NOW, before you know it, it's half time, you are two weeks along in your month quest for a new job and you are on the space marked "half time" on your job hunting calendar. So work today, except for interview appointments, to take stock of your progress.

What should you expect at this half way point? A new job? Maybe but most people don't get that job until the last week of their job search, which is still a week away. But most people are interviewing with at least one direct supervisor (which is usually the last interview) at this point and next week should bring more of these interviews.

So is your phone ringing? It should be as most employers scheduling decisive interviews contact you by phone which is more immediate and personal than the e-mail. If you phone is not ringing, check up on anyone you are expecting to hear from but has not called. I did this once to find an employer who was just getting to call me, and gave me the interview and the job. But don't "bug" an employer by calling if an e-mail (just a form of fast mail) is more appropriate or calling him twice in a day. Especially during these busy days with high unemployment—and busy employers who have many calls to answer—be mindful not to stress him with a constant need to stay in touch.

Have you been on several interviews with no apparent result? This could be because there were many other applicants to interview and they are still on their first round of interviews. Or your name may be given to another interviewer, the head of the human resources or the head of the department where the job occurs. This can take a week or more but you can call to see the progress of your interview. The receptionist may say "the job is filled," in which case you thank her and hang up. Don't argue with her, demand to know why you didn't get the job or to talk personally to the person who did not hire you. If you feel it was a good interview and it would help you to learn how you missed the job as a tool in your future job hunting, leave this message for the interviewer. Often the answer is that there was a more qualified applicant or that they were in a hurry and had to hire someone they interviewed before you. Or, course, that they are still interviewing. I did this only to find, for instance, that another teacher had children to support and needed the job worse than I did, or, sob, I didn't ace the interview or one of my references did not return their call. These things are the basis for improving your interview skills during the next two weeks, which is plenty of time for an applicant to get more interviews.

GETTING INTERVIEWS

Getting interviews is the secret of success at this half way point. If you are getting them, review them to see if they are still "alive" or if, perhaps, they failed to get you the job for whatever reason. The average person gets one interview for every 10 thoughtful applications (not blind applications to every opening available) and one job for every five last-round interviews. So the average applicant needs to make at least 50 applications for every job offer. No supervisor wants to spend any more time with applicants than necessary interviewing but will tell his human resources department to screen applicants carefully to weed out those who obviously can not do the job.

At half time you should have at least five interviews including at least one or two interviews with a supervisor with the possibility of hire. If you don't, see if you can screen jobs more carefully, are you applying for some you don't qualify for, have you slipped up on your interview techniques, are you relying on "snail mail" which takes longer for them to contact you than on the Internet? There is an answer for each interview and you should evaluate each one something like this:

Monday, Feb 7, 9 a.m.—Interview for sales position with men's department of Black and Brown Clothing Store-spoke with Mr. Black who said that successful candidates must also interview with Mr. Brown. Decision next week. (here you should check up to see if you are one of them).

Tuesday, Feb. 8, 11 a.m.—Interview with The Salvation Army Personnel Department with Captain Swift. We had a good interview but they hired the applicant interviewed on Monday because they needed to fill the job fast.

Wednesday, Feb. 9, 10 a.m.—Interview with receptionist at Friendly Law firm for secretarial job. She said the top candidates would get an interview with the senior partner next week. Check back with her next week.

Thursday, Feb. 10—Interview for receptionist position with Long Life Insurance Company who said you were "overqualified" and that your salary expectations were too high.

Friday, Feb 11—Interview with Manpower Trucking Company where the interviewer suggested you might like to continue the interview over a drink that night at the neighborhood bar. Refuse and leave.

So, which of these interviews are still alive? Certainly the Monday interview at the clothing store, and the Wednesday interview at the law office and you should definitely follow up on them. Two live interviews in two weeks is about par for the course, remember you spent a day "getting over it" and a day signing up for benefits at the state employment office and on your application blank and resume. And it takes a while to get things started.

Learn from the lessons of Tuesday, Thursday and Friday by trying to sense when an employer has a lot of applicants, is in a rush to hire, when you are overqualified for the position and where there might be less than a gentlemanly response to your interview. And take satisfaction that the men's clothing company and law firm are still in the running.

VISUALIZE YOUR "PERFECT JOB"

Now, just sit back and visualize what your "perfect job" might be. You are much better prepared to do this now than you were at the beginning of your job search because you have had your taste of interviewing, you have met a variety of supervisors in different settings and you know what is really possible for you. So here are some of the things you may want in this "perfect job."

- Good pay
- Employee benefits including health care
- A job that begins soon
- A job close to home to cut down on commute
- A job with someone really good to work with
- A job you really can handle

72

- A job in a field you really care about

- A job with a future and possible promotion

- A job with a company that is stable and not laying off workers

So, now how do the jobs with the clothing store and law firm stack up? If both of them pay $2,000 a month with benefits and will begin soon, then your choice will be more for the person, company, field and stability of the job as well as its location close to home. In this case, say, the law firm is local and close to home and the clothing company is in the nearest city a half hour away on the freeway from you. This is an advantage for the law firm. You haven't met the lawyer yet but you liked the receptionist and you still have to meet Mr. Brown but you liked Mr. Black, so score this one even. Both jobs have a future, the law firm can make you a paralegal and the clothing company can make you a department head—which do you prefer? And neither company is laying off workers and has been in business for over 10 years so they are both stable.

So, at this point, you want both of them, perhaps equally until you meet your immediate supervisor, so pursue both of them. Stay in touch with the receptionist and Mr. Black to see when your next interview might be and go on it. After that, you probably will know which job you want most and they will know which applicant they want. Then, if Mr. Black needs time to talk with Mr. Brown but the lawyer can make the decision on his own and does so on the interview, Bingo! You have the job you want.

IF YOU AREN'T SO LUCKY

Of course if you have no "live interviews" at half time or are faced with choices of jobs you really don't want, get a whole new mind set. Take another look at the openings before you and see if you can decipher from what is said in the ad what the outcome might be. The ad for the clothing store might have indicated interviews with both Mr. Brown and Mr. Black, the Salvation Army might be talking about "need for an immediate hire" for their job, the insurance company might have indicated minimum qualifications like "answering the phone, typing 45 wpm," etc., and the trucking company might have indicated an industrial environment or need for working under stress. Avoid these things on future contacts.

DON'T GO IT ALONE

Half time is a good time to network with others who are looking for a job to compare strategies and see if you are in tune with the flow of other applicants during these busy times. Don't be afraid that by sharing your contacts or success you are "helping the competition." You are all in the same boat and the worst enemy of all is doing nothing and operating in a vacuum. You should have some social life every work day outside the formal job hunting process and talking with others in the Employment Department line, at lunch at the corner café, on the bus or with a stranger at night at a local bar often opens up new ideas and procedures that will add not only to getting a job in a month but a job you really want.

Your job coach at the state employment office may be able to offer suggestions as to which type of openings might be best for you, be soonest to hire, have the most friendly offices, or the best chance for promotion. If you are unsure about how long it will take to commute, parking or how pleasant the job site, take an exploratory trip there and see. Or combine two or three job sites on the same trip, timing your trip and keeping track of how many miles round trip and your gas. If public transportation is involved, get a schedule and map from your local transit company and make this trip as well, keeping track of the time each way, cost of parking at the transit station, cost of tickets and how long it takes to get there. These days many applicants will give up to $5 an hour for a job close to home (saving transportation time and money) and cutting down on the stress connected with just getting to work each day. I was one of those and accepted the job with the lawyer because it was five minutes from home with free parking and virtually no gas consumption. Others, with more demanding cost of living expenses, may be forced to commute a half hour to the nearest city where the company may or may not offer parking, free or at no charge, and rush hour traffic cause long and unpredictable delays.

KEEP UP YOUR MORALE

One danger in taking time off for assessment at half time is to allow yourself to feel depressed and experience a return of the "woe is me" you may have felt on your first day of job search. You may not have a job yet but you are halfway there and the most fun parts—like deciding which job offer to accept—are ahead of you. There are certainly some positive things about your job search so far so concentrate on them and accentuate the positive. No one wants to talk with an applicant so down on his luck that all he can do is beg for a job. Begging can be done at your local food bank, employers are looking for confident, positive employees. Because they want to work with confident, positive people. If nothing else, the fact that you have stayed with your schedule for two weeks is reason to feel good—sadly, the majority of job applicants today do not. By now they have found reason to take a day off, to cancel an interview simply because they don't feel like talking today or purposely ruining a job interview because they don't need this one, anyway.

Get back with it and go over your strong job points. They may be:

- You are qualified for the job

- You have good experience in the job
- You really are interested in the jobs you are applying for
- You interview well, you have the gift of gab
- You like the salary or job benefits
- You are good looking and dress well
- You can find something to like about anyone you talk with and can get a good interview from even the most grumpy interviewer
- You are persistent by nature and never give up
- You know you will have a new job at the end of the month and interview with that expectation

You should be qualified and have experience for the jobs you seek because that is covered in this book. You can get the gift of gab by practicing your interviews and interviewing often, you can make the most of any salary and benefits because they are better than being unemployed, if you have personal charisma, be aware of it but don't count on it as it is taken for granted after you are on the job awhile, even with an interviewer who is tired or grumpy, you can talk him up, thus making it a pleasant experience for you, at least. If you are persistent, prove it by following every lead through to the job you want. And have confidence you will have a job by the end of your job search, ending the need to apply for jobs next season or next year, for instance.

No matter how good or poor your half time assessment is, you still have half of the job hunt before you and can learn from this process, if only that all of the jobs you are seeking are not interesting, or perhaps they are interesting but they don't pay enough or that you need to do a more careful job of scheduling your time so you make more progress in your second half. Any way you look at it, like a good coach and his team, observing half time is necessary and can be the key to your success.

START YOUR SECOND HALF

Your second half should be easier and more fun than the first half. After all, you are done with the tedious process of filling out application blanks and resumes (yours are already in your folder ready for distribution) and you are getting the hang of interviewing. It's more fun to talk with people in person than on the phone or through the Internet and you can just feel success coming on.

Most people do get a job offer between the third and fourth weeks, so this is just a week away. The very thought of it is encouraging and should raise your level of enthusiasm and confidence. Keep on keeping on and you WILL have a job, and one you want, at the end of the month.

You must, however, contact prospective employers daily by Internet, want ads, openings at the employment office and whatever other source is good for you. And don't forget your responsibilities to report in to the employment office. You can't allow anything, even an interview with a job you really want, to interfere with a required trip to the employment office. The employment office, after all, is the one paying you this week. Good employers interested in you, will usually reschedule if you ask them well ahead of time and don't wait until the day of the interview or just before the interview is scheduled because that employer may well feel you are habitually late for work or just don't show.

So schedule any new interviews you may have carefully, allowing plenty of time between them, so you don't have to hurry from one to the other, creating stress, or be even a few minutes late for any of them. I usually schedule at least two hours between interviews in the same area and even more if they are in different suburbs or towns. A quick exploratory trip to the job site will tell you how much time you need. And if an employer needs to re-schedule, do so pleasantly because this quality is pleasing to busy employers. The lawyer I worked for was popular because anytime another attorney or a judge had to reschedule for any reason, he always said, "No problem. Let me give you my secretary who will reschedule that for you," showing confidence in my ability to handle the job and also leaving the details to his support staff. He was always friendly and flexible so when he retired and it was time for me to look for another job, other lawyers looked at my resume saying, "So you worked with the Friendly Law Firm. I liked working with them. When would you like to begin?"

Now look at all the contacts and interviews you have scheduled. Using the list of things you want most in a job, rate each one according to your ability to perform the job, salary and benefits, etc. Come out with a 1, 2 or 3 rating for each, even if you must rely only on information on the Internet or in the newspaper. By now you know how to interpret "immediate hire" "no experience necessary" "salary open" "good company benefits," etc. Proceed from initial contacts to accepting interview appointments for jobs ranking highest on this list. Within the 1 ratings, try to rate the job you want most, the next most, etc. Begin to visualize yourself with this job.

For the two remaining jobs with the clothing company and the lawyer, for instance, they might rank the same except for location which would be in favor of the lawyer in your home town. And, even if you have yet to talk to your immediate supervisor, how did you like the people you did talk to? Was the receptionist friendly and in her way as authoritative as the clothing store partner (she did call your references) or was she so busy typing up a pleading that she hardly noticed you? Was the partner in the clothing store friendly and did he go into depth in your interview or did he seem to leave everything to a partner you have not met yet. Do both of them indicate a final interview on the same day or is this final interviewer out of town, busy talking to other applicants or otherwise unable to talk with you soon?

Be sure your references are answering their phones and have good things to say about your, For many employers, checking your references is the last step before offering you the job, like the polygrapher and the clothing store. Sometimes the holdup before a last interview is that the references were out of town, did not answer or had something less than positive to say about you. You can always ask if a company has heard from your references, never asking what was said. They may say they are still contacting references or that yours have responded or that they no longer want to talk with you, which may mean that your references are not cooperating. You should call your references and see if they have been contacted and if there is more information you can give them. In rare instances, they will say they have nothing to say about you besides the required dates of employment or that they really can't give you a good reference. At this point revise your resume to show these as previous employers only, not as references which are supposed to have something good in depth to say about you. Don't allow an unenthusiastic reference to cost you the job you want.

Sometimes you are confronted with a questionable reference during the final interview. Even the polygrapher, who generally raved about me, was honest and said "she talks a little too much." I got the job with the lawyer anyway and he shared this information with me only over lunch after I had "made it" with his firm. The polygrapher, after all, could not tell a lie and I continue to talk a little too much.

Contact both the lawyer's receptionist and the receptionist at the clothing store to see if they have another interview for you. And if they both do, go to both of them, open for whatever may happen. A second interview or an interview with your actual supervisor is your top priority because this is where an employer decides which applicant gets the job and sometimes makes the offer on the spot in which case you must be prepared to get all the information you need about salary, etc., what time you are to come to work and give a definite acceptance so as not to leave your future employer guessing. This is no time for "I want to sleep on it" or "I'll let you know tomorrow" as you should have thought about this before this crucial interview.

Before that last interview, study up on the company, "Goggle" them on the Internet, ask the Better Business Bureau about the company, visit the company site for any information you may need such as whether they have a parking lot, a company cafeteria, a lobby or room to relax in on breaks, how large are their work spaces (if in open view by the public) and the mood at closing time (do they go home or stay working overtime?) Often friends, family or other applicants have experience with these companies and they have ads or community service features on television, Have you been a customer, used their service or product, do you even care about what they do or make (it's hard to sound interested in a job you don't care about).

Now, before the interview if possible, try again to rate these jobs. Say you really are more interested in the lawyer because it's close to home and you have always been intrigued by the law, having seen Perry Mason and other shows involving lawyers. Or you are more interested in the clothing company because you like clothes and take pride in dressing well. You can not make up your mind about either job because you have yet to meet the person who will be your supervisor but you can size up other factors, giving them some priority in your interview schedule.

So put your interviews in some sort of order and, allowing for the possibility of being hired on the spot, go to your best job first. So if the lawyer does offer you the job and you like him, you can accept because with other things being equal (even if you might like Mr. Brown) the lawyer had the better deal in the first place. But if the lawyer doesn't offer you the job, go in to see Mr. Brown with the freedom to accept that job if you like him. The lawyer (or any other supervisor) may have other good applicants to interview or just lack the spontaneity or confidence to hire you on the spot.

Say both the lawyer and Mr. Brown say they have other applicants to interview and a couple days later one or the other calls you with a job offer. And say that you really prefer the lawyer but Mr. Brown calls you first. What do you say? Do you say you have another employer you want to check with first? Applicants don't have this advantage these days. You will have to give some answer to Mr. Brown who may be your next employer and at the same time give yourself a chance to check in with the lawyer if you really prefer him. You can say you just need to check on something, can you call him later the same day? Usually he will say yes, if it's the same day and he doesn't have to wait too long to hear from you. Then pick up the phone, call the lawyer and say you have another job offer but you would prefer to work for him. The lawyer may say he hasn't made up his mind or he was just getting ready to call you and offer you the job. Accept the job or decide if you will wait for him and risk losing the job with the clothing store. In any case, tell the lawyer to stay in touch with you and call Mr, Brown back with a final answer. In today's economy you will take the sure hire with Mr. Brown but you should be sure that you at least want this job. If the lawyer calls you later with a job offer, you will know more about how you like working with Mr. Brown and if you like it, decline the lawyer who will understand he lost you to his own indecision in hiring. If you find you just don't like working with the clothing store and are wishing you were with the lawyer, just accept the job with the lawyer, giving the clothing company your apology and regrets, companies do this to applicants all the time. And they have a list of other applicants, recently interviewed, who need the job and will be happy to work with them. Never let you fear of leveling with an employer or turning down a job you don't want at this stage interfere with accepting the job you really want. Once during better times, I was offered a counseling job with Planned Parenthood, a receptionist job for a travel company, and a job as an assistant teacher at a high school. I took the high school job because I had been a teacher once and wanted to return to this profession. Planned Parenthood and the travel company had other applicants interested in working for them and made quick hires, leaving me with not only a good job, but a choice of good places to work in.

TESTING, TESTING, TESTING

One of the necessary evils for many jobs is testing. Most applicants enjoy this about as much as a trip to the dentist's office and cringe at the thought of a machine or some interviewer's test being the measure of his ability to work.

I must say I'm one of them but I also recognize the necessity of testing, especially for government jobs or jobs where large numbers people are to be hired, leaving the employer with the need for some sort of instrument to screen the many people seeking every job he has.

So tests are a "necessary evil" and you should be prepared for them. Some tests are even interesting, appear harmless and can even be entertaining if you relax and go with the flow. Some tests are obviously useless and a few are even "illegal" at least according to ethical personnel standards.

One test which you should not take and beware of a company that uses it, is the Minnesota Multaphasic Inventory, which was developed and standardized on mental patients. You are not a mental patient and should not be judged by these standards so, if asked to take one, share this information with the employer, who honestly may not know it, and ask to skip the test.

Other legitimate tests included the dreaded typing test (especially in jobs like the law office), general knowledge, English and math tests (an employer has a right to expect his employees to add and subtract and to write an understandable sentence), physical agility tests for those in the trades, or a test drive for a delivery position. I had to take a typing test at the Friendly Law Firm and noticed stickers with the letters on the keys were in place on a keyboard too worn out to see the letters clearly. This seemed strange to me since we type by touch so I asked the receptionist why there were there. "We didn't test the last secretary who needed to see the letters on the keys," the receptionist said," so we at least want our next one to type." This office had, perhaps, been too friendly and trusted this applicant, actually recommended by another lawyer in town, on one of the most important qualifications for the job but they found out about it the first day. In this case I was glad I took the typing test so my employer wouldn't have to worry about me, too.

Typing from a dictaphone is one of the old-school testing hangovers for attorneys, polygraphers and other supervisors who don't want to pay a secretary just to sit down and take a letter in shorthand. Pleadings and long reports are also done this way when the "dictator" wants to be alone to gather his thoughts. So, if you are looking in these fields, master the dictaphone, just try it a few times before you take the test. Another time-honored skill in law offices, especially, is shorthand—either Greg or something that will let you get your supervisor's thoughts down quickly as the inspiration comes to him. The Friendly Law office liked shorthand because the lawyer was interested in his secretary's reaction to his letter and even would ask for a reaction before finishing the session. I was made to feel part of the team and on non sensitive matters like form I clients or "you need to pay your bill" letters to clients, he trusted me to say it my way, freeing himself up for more important matters. I also was told I needed to pass the state Notary Public exam as part of my job because we notarized documents for our clients, even when he was not in the office. I had a month to take and pass the exam, which I did and upon which I received my health benefits.

Many companies give standard achievement tests to all their employees. Achievement tests measure academic achievement, mainly in language and mathematics, with some questions involving logic and spatial perception. One favorite is the Wonderlic, a twelve-minute, two page flip over general test of some 75 questions which no applicant I have ever met scored perfectly in the time allowed. The questions involve things like choosing words that mean the same or opposite, the meaning of old sayings ("like father, like son") and piecing together parts of squares and triangles, word and mathematical problems. Now we recognize this is not fair to baby-boomers who may not have been schooled in Mother Goose and other wise sayings and overly fair to English and math majors. But it does standardize out surprising well in separating the really sharp from the rather dull applicants. Most employers who use these take them with a grain of salt and pay attention only to the very high or very low scores.

Some warehouse, construction and even office jobs ask an applicant to enter the job situation and perform for a short time. This bothers many applicants who get stage fright or even feel insulted that they should be asked to perform for free. But look upon this as an opportunity to experience the actual working situation, including your work area, the conditions that aid or prevent work, and the mood of the people you may be working with. In a small office, you get this in the interview, in the same office and with the same people you will be working with. In a large company, this works to your advantage as well as the company's.

Some personality tests, short of the Minnesota Multaphiasic Inventory (the MMPI) are valid or at least ethical and some companies still use them. I would rather trust an interview with my supervisor to check things out but some companies use these to get a better picture of an applicant, especially if they are unsure of their interview effectiveness. Some of these personality tests are straight forward and simple, such as those which ask if you would rather be an engineer or a fireman, or check on your favorite leisure activities. Be honest on these, but remember that employers are usually suspicious of extreme answers. If you find yourself answering things that do not seem characteristic of the people in the office you see, maybe you are not the type of person who should work there. But do not let fear of losing a job lead you to falsify your answers. It would be worse to have them hire you thinking that you are a team player and "one of them" only to find out you are a loner and don't take part in any company activities.

There are, of course, more tests but these are the main ones. And tests are one of the things that can be determined in other ways and delay your job acceptance so generally steer away from them if you can.

WORKING WITH AGENCIES

You can't go it alone and from the beginning you need to work at least with your State Employment Office. This is necessary to qualify for benefits and today with many government jobs available, this can be an "inside line" to one of these jobs. They are the first outside help you need and you should contact them on your first day to sign up for unemployment benefits, now worth about half of you net paycheck. Don't be too proud to ask the government for help, after all, you have been paying taxes for this service all your working life. You have a right to help from State Employment so do this in a polite and professional way.

They are very busy these days with the many unemployed so be patient and appreciative of their service. Stand in line, sign up for a phone consultation or apply by Internet if requested and take time to say "thank you" to these conscientious and overworked employees. When I did this, they usually paused and smiled, a little surprised than any anxious applicant would take the time or show any gratitude for simple service. That moment probably made no difference in my day, they were helping me as fast and as well as they could, but it made a difference in theirs.

The way you work with State Employment varies from state to state, but all require you to sign up, report in the office regularly and fill out questionnaires about jobs you are seeking and your progress, including any jobs accepted or rejected. Here be warned that refusal of a job that is deemed right for you may result in loss of your benefits. Here you can not afford to be choosy about where you work or to refuse a job that is "beneath you" if the pay is what you need and you can handle it. Personality conflict is no reason for you not to accept a job and may not be sufficient reason for you to collect benefits if YOU are the one to leave the job. But if you suffer through the conflict and make it necessary for a company to fire you then you should receive benefits because you did everything you could to keep the job.

Better to nip this in the bud by not pursuing a job with a supervisor that you know you can't get along with. Like the employer who asked me to continue my interview over cocktails that night. Sexual harassment, or enticement, is illegal and you are within your rights to refuse to accept a job with that employer. One employer of one of my clients noticed her flirting with him, smiling widely and perhaps looking for an invitation to that evening cocktail. This employer, who was not wearing a wedding ring, asked her "Say, are you married?" She pointed out her wedding ring, saying "Yes, I am." "I am too, darn it," he said gently letting her know that it was a professional, not a personal relationship, they were talking about. She caught on immediately, said

"Of course," stopped flirting, tightened up her interview and got the job.

The Internet is really an agency, you are working with Yahoo, Hot Mail or whatever company is managing the web site. You are required to sign some sort of agreement with the company not to reproduce or sell their material and they are obliged to keep your sensitive information confidential. This is a most important aid discussed in an earlier chapter but you should understand here you are working with an agency and have certain reasonable expectations and responsibilities.

OTHER AGENCIES

Most other agencies you will encounter on the job search are private agencies and "head hunters." I worked for Snelling and Snelling, at the time the franchise of the largest employment agency in the country). The owners were also a church-based couple which played to my advantage. They said they never hired "goody, goody" church people but would take a chance with me. I learned that they were very "applicant friendly" and that my philosophy fit in well with theirs. I learned many things in this job including that an agency, while financially motivated, can be of real help to an applicant, especially one that is making slow progress on his own or is pursuing a high paying or professional job where openings might not be available in other sources.

Here it is still usually possible to take a "no fee" job, one for which the employer will pay the fee. Pursue these first because at least the employer is serious enough to risk some money on you. And, in jobs for which applicants are hard to find or hard to screen, an agency can be the ideal go-between. Many law firms, business and financial firms and employers in fields that demand confidentiality or the use of "inside information" use agencies to screen out the friendly from the introverted, the honest from the dishonest, the discreet from the babblers. I got a job as secretary the senior partner of a successful law firm specializing in family law with an agency and found myself interviewing with a high school buddy of my supervisor at the Friendly Law Firm and, upon realizing this connection, the new lawyer said—yes— "When you like to start?" When this senior partner retired, I got another interview purely at random, with a university buddy of my Friendly Law Firm lawyer and when he heard I had been working with his buddy said—yes—"When you like to start?" I liked both of them as much as the original "friendly" lawyer and we I have had occasion to do business with both of them, even after I left their offices for other jobs.

Agencies, however, are disappearing now with the financial crisis and some are demanding outrageous fees for their services. Study their contracts carefully and ask any questions you may have—or take it home with you—before signing something you cannot afford or can do on your own. Be wary of an agency or "head hunter" which charges you a fee. The employer is better able to pay a fee and should be willing to do it if he values you as a prospective employee.

CLOSING THE DEAL

Now you are almost there. It is the fourth week of your job hunting schedule, you have good interviews this week and you're bursting with confidence and enthusiasm. It is true that most of our applicants get a job offer by this the end of this week and the odds are that if you persevere, you will be one of them. The odds are also that this offer will not come until Friday, so don't slow down or get over confident.

Take a good look at your interview schedule. You should be dealing with "fresh" jobs you have pursued since half time. Companies with long interview schedules or which have to get approval from national headquarters or from a supervisor who is out of town may well not get their act together by this Friday and this is when you want your job.

So look at this week's fresh interviews and prepare for them in the same way you have done before but with you focus on the "end game," when you will get a job offer. The employers I have worked with knew a good employee when they saw one and offered me a job during the interview, subject to checking my references. The lawyer took care of this in advance so he would be ready to hire me during the interview. The polygrapher had his wife call me as soon as my references checked because he had already made up his mind. The senior minister was a great judge of character and, trusting his junior minister, did not hesitate to endorse the work of his assistant, even with someone he just met. He was the one who invited me to lunch the next day so he could take care of this and check my references, of course.

The only really good jobs I have gotten that took a long time were in teaching where the wheels of the school board turn slowly and much paperwork seems to fly in the interim. Other jobs with large companies sometimes moved fast for me, the Snelling and Snelling job came the week of my interview because the particular franchise was owned by partners in marriage as well as in business who communicated quickly with their headquarters that they wanted to take a chance on a candidate from The Salvation Army. When I worked in that personnel office, I saw what a leap of faith this took and had a chance to peek at my competition for that job, impressive to say the least, but I was the only applicant with previous church experience.

Jobs with government, once the slowest of all, are now the fastest, with literally millions of openings to be filled. And the faster the government fills them, the faster we are employees again, paying our taxes, spending money to stabilize the economy and lightening the load of the State Employment Office. So it is to their advantage, as well as yours, to apply for these jobs, if possible at your State Employment Office. They too are eager to fill these jobs, to get you and them off their work load so they can help the next million job hunters.

So be ready to ask in so many words if an employer is actually offering you a job or just asking if you would like it, when you will begin, all information you may need about salary and benefits and if asked on the phone or person, give a definite answer. Which should be "yes" if you have done your homework correctly. If you have to refuse a job at this point because the salary is not enough, because you don't like the person you talked with or really could not work in that setting, you need to tighten up your procedure to see that these things are asked before the time of acceptance. However, if the company just has not said exactly what the salary or benefits are or if you have yet to meet the person who will be your supervisor, take care of this before accepting a job. Let's go over this most important time of your job hunt—and listen in on how you close the deal with various employers.

POLYGRAPHER'S WIFE
Hello, Suzy. This is Helen Thompson with Tompson Polygraphing where you met my husband this week.

SUZY
Yes, I met him last on Wednesday.

POLYGRAPHER'S WIFE
Well, he enjoyed talking with you and your references had some good things to say about you. So we are offering you the job.

SUZY
That's great!

POLYGRAPHER'S WIFE
(needing a definite answer)
But do you accept?

SUZY (catching on)
Yes, I accept and I think that's great.

POLYGRAPHER'S WIFE
Did he tell you about the salary and benefits?

SUZY
Yes, half time for $10 an hour.

POLYGRAPHER'S WIFE
Yes, we will pay you 20 hours a week whether we need you for that long or not as we have an irregular schedule and need you when we have testing. There are no health benefits now but we're working on it and you get the state paid holidays off since we work a lot with public agencies. I hate to ask you on such short notice but we need to get started next week so can you come in for some training tomorrow at 9 o'clock?

SUZY
(Pausing because she promised to meet her
daughter's plane at 9:30)
Well, my daughter is flying in from St. Louis that
morning for a visit but my husband can meet her. Yes,
I will be there at 9.

POLYGRAPHER'S WIFE
(grateful for a meeting on short notice)
Thank you for being so flexible. I look forward to
seeing you tomorrow morning and I'll have the coffee
pot on.

SUZY
Thank you. I'll see you then.

LET'S LOOK AT IT
Suzy needed some help with the salary and
benefits—she was happy to know she was
guaranteed 20 hours a week because sometimes
there was not 20 hours of work to do and she was
paid anyway. And she failed to ask about health
benefits, which the polygrapher's wife made sure that
she understood they offered none but were
considering it. Suzy was able to think on her feet on
the airport issue—some new workers might have said
that tomorrow morning was not convenient and
probably would not have lost the job since the
polygrapher really wanted her but Suzy was able to

do what happened often in their house—one spouse meets the family of either spouse who is otherwise occupied and make a good first impression.

MR. BROWN AT THE CLOTHING STORE
Hello, Suzy. This is Mr. Brown at the Black and Brown Clothing Company. You talked with my partner, Mr. Black, last week.

SUZY
Yes, I did on Monday.

MR. BLACK
Well, he really enjoyed talking with you and asked me to call you.

SUZY
(Wondering what the reason for the call might be) Yes, I really enjoyed talking with him, too.

MR. BLACK
Well, I'd like to talk with you, too. How about tomorrow morning at 9?

SUZY
I'd like to but I promised to meet my daughter at the airport—she's flying in from St. Louis for a visit. (This is short notice for a second interview rather than the start of an actual job and Suzy wonders if the clothing company can reschedule.)

MR. BLACK
How about 9 o'clock on Tuesday, then?

SUZY

Thank you. I'll see you then.

LET'S LOOK AT IT

Here Suzy wanted to talk with Mr. Black but this was just a second but final) interview so she gives her reason for wanting another day and asks him to reschedule. Which he is happy to do since he is still in the interview stage and has others to interview before reaching a decision. At this rate it will be at least midweek or at the end of the fourth week before a job is awarded. He would probably be unhappy if Suzy had missed meeting her daughter's plane on speculation only, perhaps, to hire another applicant. And Suzy would certainly be unhappy if she gave this up only to lose the job.

Let's look at another "closing" interview that didn't work for the applicant. This is a call to work from the travel company where Suzy applied for a receptionist position because she loved to travel and it had travel privileges.

TRAVEL COMPANY MANAGER

Hello, Suzy. This is Sally from Wanderlust Travel Company. How are you today?

SUZY

I'm fine.

TRAVEL COMPANY MANAGER
Well, we really enjoyed meeting you the other day and we wanted you to come in.

SUZY
To work, you mean? (clarifying an important issue)

TRAVEL COMPANY MANAGER
Yes, to work mornings next week just to see how you work out. You don't have any travel experience but we liked you and think you may be just what we need at our front desk. And the lady there is leaving today so we need someone there on Monday.

SUZY
Are you offering me the job?

TRAVEL COMPANY MANAGER
Not yet. We have one other lady we would like to try out in the afternoon and we'll know by next Friday.

SUZY
Would I be paid for this?

TRAVEL COMPANY MANAGER
Yes, the regular $10 an hour, mornings half time 8-12 without benefits, of course. We will know by the end of the week if we want you or the other lady.

SUZY
So, there are two of us still in the running for the job. (pauses) Sure, I enjoyed meeting you too and I know I

would enjoy this job. I'll see you at 8 o'clock Monday morning.

OR

Thank you but I need my time to get a job and next week is critical to me. Could we take care of this in another way, with another interview?

TRAVEL COMPANY MANAGER
I wish we could but our owner wants to see you work.

SUZY
Thank you but I need next week to interview. I enjoyed talking with you and hope you find a good receptionist.

LET'S LOOK AT IT

Suzy has to decide quickly whether she can give up morning interviews for a 50% chance at a job next week. If she has some good interviews already scheduled, perhaps with better pay, she will keep to her schedule and turn down the travel company. But if she's not busy next week and really just needs this job, she may want to go in and try out, at least she will be paid and have this on-the-job experience. This is like accepting a temporary job during the job search to get some money in the bank until a job offer comes along. Which may be at the end of the week at the travel company. One of my clients, who tried out with a travel company, actually took the morning job and they gave the afternoon job to the other applicant.

This is possible if you don't need a full time job to live on and offers free time and travel privileges which are a special incentive which will probably not be given on other jobs.

Now, say, during this "trial period," the polygrapher's wife calls and wants Suzy to go to work. She's not going to say, sorry I'm trying out for a job at the travel company. Not if she's serious about getting the polygrapher's job.

How does she handle this?

POLYGRAPHER'S WIFE
Hello, Suzy. This is Helen Thompson, the wife of the polygrapher you talked with last week.

SUZY
Hello.

POLYGRAPHER'S WIFE
Well, my husband enjoyed talking with you and we'd like to offer you the job.

SUZY
That's half time at $10 an hour?

POLYGRAPHER'S WIFE
Yes, we will pay you 20 hours a week whether we need you or not so you can count on an income and we can count on you.

SUZY

That's very thoughtful. I enjoyed talking with your husband, also. When would you like me to begin?

POLYGRAPHER'S WIFE

We are going to be busy next week so we were wondering if you could come in tomorrow at 8?

SUZY

(without going into the airport issue)

Yes, thank you. I'll see you tomorrow morning.

LET'S LOOK AT IT

Here Suzy has a choice between the job she is "trying out for" at the travel company and a sure job with the polygrapher, both half time and with the same pay) but the polygrapher guarantees her an income and what amounts to time off in their quiet weeks.) Even if Suzy is already "trying out" with the travel company she is free to tell them she's sorry but she had to accept a sure job with someone else. The travel company already has the other lady they can hire if they want to, Suzy is not really letting them down and she would regret it if she turned down the polygrapher just because she was already "trying out" with someone make their minds up about which applicant to hire and avoid the unpleasant task of putting two potential employees up against each other for the job.

SEALING THE DEAL

Here we cover such things as signing agreements with the employer or an agency and the matter of trust that a job actually offered will be there when you come in to work. The vast majority of companies honor their word and the applicant should not initiate a written agreement if she does not have to. But, of course, she will follow the lead if a company insists, some companies will have an employee sign a confidentiality agreement that they will not use leads or other confidential information learned on the job after leaving. This is understandable and is used often by agencies, advertising, personnel or others that value their contacts or unique on-the-job training.

But most companies, all those discussed here except Snelling and Snelling, hired me by word of mouth and the hire was solid. Snelling and Snelling, being a franchise of the largest employment company at the time, did ask me to sign such an agreement the day I came in to work but it was a formality and one I never violated.

Some applicants feel they need security in choosing a job with the polygrapher, for instance, so they won't miss out on the travel company. Oral invitations to work are hard to prove but the Employment Development office would interview the hiring company representative and ask them if a job was offered. 99% of employers do not lie to the Employment Service and you certainly don't want to work with the other 1%. Trust that the employer really will stand behind his offer made in person or on the phone and just accept graciously. Don't ask for a written agreement if you don't need one, this only breeds distrust in what should be an enthusiastic and friendly acceptance.

KNOW WHEN IT'S OVER

After accepting a job, clear your interviews with other employers. Don't leave them waiting for you the next day and leave it for them to guess that you just aren't dependable or accepted another job. How would you feel if that employer greeted you with the news that you weren't wanted after all, because they hired someone else. Just call each employer with whom you have scheduled an interview and tell them thank you but you have just accepted another job. They will probably just wish you well and go on to the next applicant.

And don't let the feeling that you just might not work out on this new job allow you to keep an employer hanging, "I'm trying out next week at the travel company but if it doesn't work out, I'll get in touch with you." By then they will probably have hired someone else and they don't want to be your second choice, anyway.

Accept the job you have, put away this book and give yourself a small celebration. Like sleeping late the next day, taking a friend out to dinner, something quick and simple but something meaningful. Put a star on the day of the calendar on which you accepted this new job. And celebrate, celebrate, celebrate!

KEEP YOUR JOB

Prepare for your first day of work with the same care as any interview, be awake and alert, dress appropriately, get there on time and enter the job site with a low profile. After all you are new to this place and don't want to upstage other employees with "Hi, I'm Suzy, the new receptionist." Wait for someone to take charge and introduce you to the other employees.

Listen to what they have to say about themselves, don't insist on telling them your life story and get the tone of the office before talking too much or offering too much personal information. You are not "queen for a day" but the "new kid on the block" so act accordingly. A friendly office will introduce you around and show you the ropes with every polite consideration because they want you to succeed in this new job. And you will, so don't be too timid or lack confidence. Find a middle ground before showing off or being too quiet and then, just be yourself.

There is a lot to be said for being yourself in a proper unassuming way. If you portray yourself as a real "team player" with smiles and ready enthusiasm, everyone, including you, will be sorry if you are really a quiet thinker. They would enjoy a quiet, thinking person if that is what you portray yourself from the beginning. Most offices have at least one quiet thinker and this person may be the brains of the office. So be yourself, you will be happier and so will they.

Listen to what your supervisor says to you, carry a pad and take notes about the specifics of your new job so he will not have to repeat things. I have even been given a company pad and pen, an employee notebook and other aids from companies wanting to give a special welcome to new employees. Cooperate with the health exam, if there is one for insurance, and any other procedures required. Most of them benefit employees and are necessary so do this cheerfully. If you have a condition that would interfere with you work, you should have mentioned it during the interview. Then the company will accommodate you in this. This applies to health concerns as well as lack of basic qualifications to do a job, even if the company does not ask. Like the secretary who could not type at the law office, for example. These things will come out right away and companies do not like—and often dismiss— employees that have lied to them or even omitted what is clearly necessary information about health, experience, job skills, etc.

Keep up your work at your best for whatever the trial period may be. Even if a company does not specify a trial period, the first month at least, should be a time for special effort on your part and you should fulfill any job requirements still out there, like the lawyer who wanted me to pass the Notary Public exam and rewarded me with health benefits.

Keep up with you schedule of getting to work on time, taking care of your wardrobe and grooming and work as if you were winning your job day by day, as if you were "trying out" because in the eyes of your employer you just may be for the first month at least. Be consistent with your work ethic, especially until your first job review or until your employer calls you into the office to assess your progress and tell you how you are doing. This could be just a routine thing, an opportunity for a raise or a warning that you need to do better to stay.

If you have been working as hard to keep your job as you did to get it, your production will be consistent with the company expectation on hiring you and you should be well on your way to keeping your job. So take special care, especially during the early weeks and months, to keep your job so you don't have to repeat this process again next month.

SUMMARY

Now, let's summarize what we have learned in this book, arranged in order of the things you must do to get your job.

- Get over any negative feelings about losing your last job. This is "history" and you should do this in a day.
- Set up your beginning, half time day and acceptance day on your daily planner calendar. Read this book, sign up with your State Employment office and prepare your application blank and resume the second day. You can do some of this work on a notebook while waiting in the line at State Employment if necessary.
- Decide on how much you have to earn and job titles that you are able to fill.
- Start contacting employers with job openings on the Internet, in want ads, job fairs and announcements on television, at the employment office, word of mouth from friends, help wanted signs, whatever works for you. But do this EVERY DAY until you have a job. Work full time and dress for work every day, even when you don't have a scheduled interview.
- Go to any interviews you can get for jobs you can handle and which pay your bottom line. Interview, interview, interview.

- Mark you half time day with time for assessment and learning from any mistakes made during the first two weeks. Keep this day free except for interviews and contacting openings if you don't have any interviews.
- Make any changes necessary to your first two weeks in the way you make contact with employers, the way you interview or follow up. Seek the help of your Employment Development counselor, fellow job seekers, friends and family, anyone who can give you some perspective on your final two weeks of job search.
- Check back with any employers who still may want to hire you. Seek additional interviews, make sure you have their salary and benefits, indicate you are still interested in their job.
- Interview, interview, interview until you are offered a job. Be careful but clear about accepting and be sure they are really offering you a job.
- Accept your job, clear any pending interview appointments and give yourself at least a small celebration. This event of getting a new job should not pass without notice and this motivates you to keep that job.
- Keep your job so you don't have to repeat this again.

Drop me a note through my publisher to let me know what you liked, or didn't like, about this book. We will have future editions and your comments are valuable. So good luck and congratulations on your new job!

Made in the USA
Charleston, SC
02 May 2011